Choosing a Skateboard

Ali Everts

photographs by Matt Grace

Contents

Page 2	Ask an Expert
Page 4	The Deck
Page 5	The Wheels
Page 6	The Bearings
Page 7	The Trucks
Page 8	Safety Gear

Learning Media

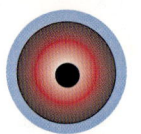

Ask an Expert

When Drew wanted to buy
a skateboard, he found there
were lots of things to think about.
Would a wide deck
be better than a narrow deck?
What kinds of wheels, bearings,
and trucks should he choose
for his skateboard?
Would he need safety gear?
He decided to ask an expert for some help.

"How do I choose a skateboard that's going to be just right for me?"

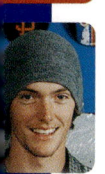

"You need to decide how much money you want to spend.
You need to think about how good you are at skateboarding and what you want your skateboard to do."

The Deck

"Can you tell me about the different decks?"

"The deck is the flat part
of the board that you stand on.
It's strong, but it'll bend,
so it won't break easily.
If you want to do flips,
then choose a skateboard
with a narrow deck.
If you want to ride on ramps
or stairs, then choose a skateboard
with a wide deck."

The Wheels

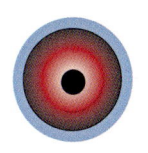

"What do I need to think about when I'm choosing wheels for my skateboard?"

"You need to decide what you're going to do on your skateboard. Small wheels are best for street boarding and flips. Big wheels are best for speed and riding in skate parks."

The Bearings

"What do I need to know about the bearings?"

"The bearings are the small, ring-shaped pieces that are filled with tiny steel balls.
They fit into the wheels and spin.
This helps the wheels to turn easily.
You need to keep the bearings clean and dry so that they don't stick."

The Trucks

"What do I need to think about when I'm choosing trucks for my skateboard?"

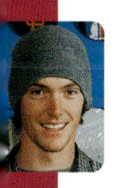

"The trucks are the T-shaped parts that join the wheels and the deck. You'll need heavy trucks for landing jumps or lighter ones for flips."

Safety Gear

"How important is safety gear?"

"Safety gear is the most important of all.
You'll need a helmet, knee and elbow
pads, and gloves.
These will help protect you
if you come off your board.
Or, I should say,
when you come off your board,
because you *will* come off.
Even the experts do that!"